The Breeder's Guide to Raising

to Raising

SUPERSTAR DOGS

JERRY HOPE, CBDC

The Breeder's Guide to Raising Superstar Dogs

"A training manual for breeders, future puppy owners, and trainers who want to influence their clients"

By Jerry Hope, CDBC

DIAMOND ~ H ~ PUBLISHING

Requests for permission to reprint from book should be sent to:

Jerry Hope E-mail – Jerry@k9fixer.com

ISBN: 978-0-615-19709-8

Editing: Anne Rogers & Ann O'Mara
Technical editing: Tammy King
Cover Photo: Mary Alice Alnutt

DIAMOND ~H~ PUBLISHING

The Breeder's Guide to Raising Superstar Dogs

This Book is Intended For.........

Breeders ~ Future Puppy Owners ~ Trainers

This book was written to help breeders prepare their pups for life in the real world so that they may reach their full potential to live happy and successful lives in our society. It is formulated to lessen any possibility that these pups could develop behavioral problems later in life. The intent of this book is to aid the breeder in achieving the dream of producing Superstar Dogs!

This book was also written to assist dog owners and future dog owners in finding the right breeder. A puppy obtained from a breeder who has subscribed to the "Superstar Program" is a puppy less likely to exhibit temperament and behavioral issues as an adult dog, and much more likely to become a stable, happy and loving family member for many years to come.

Finally, this book was written to aid trainers in advising breeder-clients on how to properly prepare a litter for success. The information provided will also enable the trainer to advise clients on how to select a quality puppy which has the best chance for success, whether as a family pet or a competition dog.

What others are saying about "Raising Superstar Dogs"

"This is a delightful book. A super book! Wonderfully well written and overflowing with numerous practical tips for raising puppies to have solid temperaments, dynamite demeanors and stellar dispositions — true SuperStar Dogs! Every breeder and every prospective puppy owner should read this book."

- Ian Dunbar PhD, BVetMed, MRCVS
  Founder of the Association of Pet Dog Trainers

"If all breeders followed Jerry Hope's Superstar Program, there would be fewer dogs in shelters, fewer behavior problems, happier owners, and many, many more well socialized dogs. In short, the world would be a better place for dogs and their people."

- Nicole Wilde, CPDT, author Help *for Your Fearful Dog* and *So You Want to be a Dog Trainer*

"People who are breeding dogs who are not properly educating the puppies or who allow puppies to leave their mother at too young an age do everyone a disservice. The problem is people still get puppies from these sources because they do not know any better. This book is an excellent source for puppy-buyers to educate themselves about what a good breeder should be providing. "

- Brenda Aloff, Midland, MI –Author of *Getting Connected With Your Dog*; *Canine Body Language, A Photographic Guide*; *Aggression in Dogs: Practical management, Prevention & Behaviour Modification* and *Positive Reinforcement: Training Dogs in the Real World*

"Jerry's love of our canine companions and his extensive experience with dogs has resulted in him producing a wonderful read full of information that should be implemented by all dog breeders. His passion for this topic shines through and having met his four-legged friends I can vouch that they are indeed 'Superstar Dogs!'"

- Tammie King Bsc (Hons) Zoologist and Dog Behaviourist, Melbourne, Australia

The Breeder's Guide to Raising Superstar Dogs

Contents

Will you PLEASE turn over and STOP snoring!

Foreword

So often, we hear "let your pup be a puppy." "Enjoy your pup and show it lots of love and it will love you in return." There is nothing better than enjoying a pup and letting him be a pup, and certainly, you should love your dog; but raising a good well-behaved dog is far more than just this. We often do not realize the stages of development a dog goes through, or if we do, we overlook them and forget to work with them to develop our perfect companion or working dog. Stages in development and learning begin the moment the pup is born. This book has brought back to me the realization of how important it is to not only know the stages a dog goes through in a very short time but how these stages affect his development, personality, temperament, working ability, behavior, and companionship.

By understanding exactly what is happening in a dog's mind and how his behavior is shaped in the unique growth stages, we can overcome so many problems and bring out the strengths we desire to raise the dog we dream of.

I am often asked, "When do I start training a pup?" My answer is the moment I pick him up, and that for me is at about 8 weeks. If I have a litter, my answer is the moment they come out of the mother's womb. I am constantly holding, watching, reading, listening, building my knowledge of each pup and noticing what we can do to create a wonderful companion. By understanding the stages of development we can interpret what is actually happening and do simple exercises, introduce certain stimuli to help the dog gain mental and physical strengths to deal with the life ahead, and be a good well behaved and balanced dog.

In this book, Jerry Hope explains the importance and responsibilities of being a good breeder. How we as breeders can bring on the perfect puppy from which owners can then build their Super Star dog. Whether you are seeking a working dog and or the perfect best friend companion, this book provides you with the basis of understanding of how your dog will and can learn so much in the first formative most important months of his developing life. The important months where habits and behaviors can and will be developed that will last a lifetime.

To call this book a breeders guide does not do the amount of information and common sense advice held within these pages justice. This is a book for everyone thinking of owning a dog, already owning a dog and those wishing to develop a wonderful companion. By building a solid foundation of behavior and brainpower in a pup we have a solid base from which to train and grow. To understand your dog and help him become a responsible canine citizen others admire is more than just rewarding, it brings a partnership and love that lasts for a lifetime. In the Chapters of this book, there is a wealth of practical common sense and fun interactions with your pup that will have you understanding, guiding and enjoying your pup and in doing so will help you create that rich human/canine bond we all long for.

Martin Deeley IACP CDT
Co-Founder, International Association of Canine Professionals
UK Gundog Trainer of the Year 2007
Author, *Working Gun Dogs, An Introduction to Training and Handling*

Gamegards Tomb Raider ~ 8 weeks old

Dedication

For most of my adult life I have been involved in the dog industry. When I was not training, I was at a show. When I was not at a show, well you get the picture; most of you reading this probably fall into the same category. For this reason, I wanted to take a moment to recognize a few of the dogs who have contributed to my success in this business. This book is dedicated to my Superstar dogs. Without them, this book would not have been possible.

To Marilyn, from the moment I first saw you, I belonged to you. You epitomize what a show dog should be. Not only did you look the part of a show dog, you had enough attitude for several Basenjis.

- 18 -

Your warm cheerful greeting every morning soothed my soul. Your bright shining face made me smile. You were the best snuggle-buddy anyone could have ever had. My world is not the same without you. "Your candle burned out long before your legend ever did."

To Kyra, my Malinois- you showed me just how big a heart a dog can have. You came to me from a place where you were not wanted; you were said to be untrainable, very destructive and riddled with stomach problems that would never be cured. You did not give up on people and you gave me a chance to prove everyone wrong. As you lie calmly on my living room floor chewing on your squeaky Kong® I know those naysayers were wrong. You will always have a place in my heart.

Finally, and this is the hardest to address, Jessie- I don't know where to begin,...I can't explain you to anyone who has never had a "heart dog," and those who have, need no explanation. You are THE standard by which I will compare all Rottweilers. You were my protector, my partner, and most of all, my best friend. I will always miss you.

Acknowledgements

There are so many people I have to thank for helping me to turn my passion into my career. Few people have the opportunity to truly and deeply love their chosen profession. To all who read this, I hope you find the caliber of people in your life that I have the fortune to have in mine. I would like to thank publicly just a few of the great dog people I've had the pleasure of associating with and have the honor to call my friends.

First, let me thank Dr. Ian Dunbar for his "tutoring from afar" for many years. Ian, you wrote about things others were afraid to even think. Some years later, when I had the honor of meeting you in person and you became my friend, I realized I didn't know just how wise you really are. Thank you for all you've done, not only for me personally, but for everything you have done for our dogs and for trainers everywhere!

I would also like to thank Tammie King. Tam, though I've only known you a short while, you have been such an inspiration to me. How can anyone be around you for more than five minute and not be inspired?

Many thanks to thank Lynn Hoover. Lynn, your help getting me involved with, what was then your organization, the International Association of Animal Behavior Consultants (IAABC) has been a great asset to my career. Furthermore, when I set out to write and publish this book, you were there with sound wisdom and timely advice. You never judged or told me what I should do. You always presented choices, allowing me to make my own decision. I just hope someday I can repay you.

Next, I want to thank Anne Rogers. Anne, you supported this book even when it was nothing more than an abstract thought. Your editing turned my southern vocabulary into something people could read and understand. Our friendship goes much further than this book, and that's what I want to thank you for the most!

I must also thank Martin Deeley. Martin, the entire dog world owes you a hardy "thank you" for your contributions to dog trainers as well as all that you have done for dogs. You are a true diplomat; your calm attitude makes you an easy person to talk to about any subject. You exude professionalism; you have such a natural ability with dogs; you should be the model that every dog trainer strives to emulate.

The Breeder's Guide to Raising Superstar Dogs

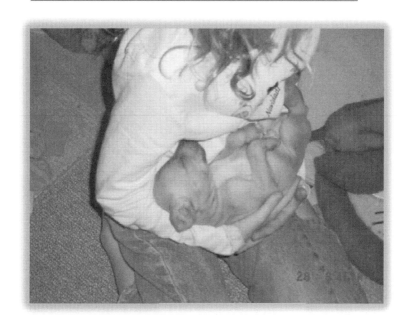

"A training manual for breeders, future puppy owners, and trainers who want to influence their clients"

By Jerry Hope, CDBC

Introduction

Each year thousands of dogs are put to an early death because they have developed behavioral problems that render them incapable of fitting into our society. Politicians have tried to solve the problem to no avail; animal shelters across the country are overrun.

Breed bans continue to pop up. Regardless of how many cities pass them they will not solve the problem. As a breeder, I feel that it is time to address this issue. This book will attack the problem head-on. Our primary weapon is the "Superstar Program," which is designed to produce dogs that can cope with and adapt to the situations they face in our society; dogs who can become the family pet that fits in; dogs whose behavior is rewarded by the owner's desire for the pleasure of the company of "man's best friend" rather than the despair of sending to a shelter or euthanizing a dog no longer view as a beloved pet but as a behavior problem.

Dogs end up in shelters for a number of reasons, many of which could have been prevented through proper early training by the owner, and more importantly, by the breeder. The "Superstar Program" is designed to do just that. Breeders have a greater impact than any other group on many of the problems that face the dog world today. Breeders choose the genetics of the dogs of tomorrow; breeders have the first and the best opportunity to prepare puppies for life; and breeders choose the persons with whom these puppies will live. Because the breeder makes these decisions and has these opportunities, the breeder has the ability to prevent many of the common behavior problems that trainers normally see; some of which may lead to the dog's demise.

In 1965, John Paul Scott and John L. Fuller published *Dog Behavior: The Genetic Basic*, (also published as *Genetics and the Social Behavior of the Dog*) which is now recognized as a landmark scientific work. Scott and Fuller showed us that the socialization periods are extremely critical, that if certain stimuli are not introduced in the first five or six weeks of life and other protocols are not initiated and carried out prior to ten weeks, psychological damage will result with little or no chance of full recovery.

We have had access to the research of Scott & Fuller for over forty years, yet very few breeders appear to have benefited from it. The primary reason for this is that until now the information has not been available in a format that could be easily understood and implemented by the average "non-scientific" person. The purpose of this book is to present that information, along with over three decades of personal experience, in a format that is easy to follow and put into practice.

Many breeders with the best of intentions produce puppies, love them, and spend a great deal of time with them. However, without the proper education, the result is a litter of puppies, which loves only THAT particular family in THAT specific environment, and under the conditions to which it has been accustomed.

Our failure as breeders and informed consumers has been costly. With the information provided in this book, I believe that we can change that, that we can make a difference. By educating the dog public with solid facts regarding the puppy's growth patterns and what should be expected during these periods, we can greatly reduce the risk that many dogs will face.

New puppy buyers also need to know what the breeder should do to prepare the puppy for life. The choice of a puppy whose breeder has utilized the techniques described in this book will not only make the new owner's task of raising the puppy much easier, it will also give the puppy a much greater chance of living a full and happy life as well as giving joy to those humans who share that life.

The three most important factors that influence a puppy's development are genetics, nutrition, and the environment. Bookshelves are full of wonderful books written specifically to cover the genetic issues. The one point I want to make here is that even the best socialization cannot compensate for poor temperament. As important as I believe socialization to be, breeding animals with poor temperaments is the most detrimental thing we can do to our breeds. Breeding dogs that are likely to pass on physical defects or a genetic predisposition to illnesses that may shorten their lives is bad enough. This causes pain, both for the dog and for the family, but rarely does it cause physical injury to humans. Breeding dogs with poor temperaments many times does just that.

The subject of nutrition is also well documented. There are too many protocols and formulas for me even to scratch the surface on that subject. It is unlikely that anyone who is reading this book and is truly interested in  improving the quality of their puppies would have overlooked the importance of proper nutrition. If you have questions as to which protocol is best for your dogs, consult your veterinarian.

Finally, trainers can use this information to predict when a pup will experience particular problems and can formulate training plans to head these problems off well before they arise.

No breeder sets out to breed a dog that he knows will not fit into our society, who will be a nuisance or who will end up being euthanized. When we breeders choose to take the reproduction functions of dogs into our own hands, we must accept the responsibility that comes with that choice. This book will illustrate how the breeder can fulfill his responsibility to produce canines with superstar qualities; pups that will become confident, outgoing individuals who can adapt to new environments with ease – dogs who are indeed "Superstars."

SECTION ONE

Critical Periods

Simply stated, the Superstar Program outlined in this book focuses on recognizing the puppy's vital mental growth periods. The lessons appropriate to each period are two-fold. It is our goal to promote the learning of desirable behaviors while avoiding the learning and reinforcement of negative behaviors. By focusing on the development of desirable behaviors, we provide a positive foundation for other life skills.

These vital mental growth periods are called Critical Periods. As the words "vital" and "critical" suggest, it is essential that the puppy's learning experiences occur at the time when optimum retention will take place. It is also most important to introduce learning experiences when the puppy is developmentally ready. Exposing a puppy to a situation, which might have a positive effect when he is a few weeks older can do a great deal of damage if he has not yet reached the appropriate level of readiness.

Fortunately we have a timeline to guide us and give us specific information regarding the developmental stages or critical periods through which the puppy progresses. As noted earlier, Scott and Fuller were among the first to define these critical periods. Their findings, based on thirteen years of research utilizing hundreds of dogs, have shown us what the pup is experiencing mentally, emotionally, and physically during the various critical periods and enables us to prepare our socialization and training programs accordingly. Since the critical periods are the foundation on which the Superstar Program is built, a clear and comprehensive understanding of these periods is most important.

Pre-natal
~ Last three weeks of pregnancy – birth

Patience is our most important tool during this period. Our goal is to keep the bitch as relaxed and calm as possible. Stress should be avoided at all costs. We need to be sure that she has adequate amounts of food containing the correct nutritional requirements (check with your veterinarian for a suitable diet) and that she has plenty of fresh, clean water. Moderate exercise is also desirable. Finally, be aware that the bitch may become quite "clingy" as her whelping date approaches. If so, indulge her need for attention and affection.

Neo-natal Period
~ Birth – 12 days

During the first weeks of life, the pups are going to spend most of their time nursing and sleeping. They should show rapid growth, perhaps even doubling their birth weight by the end of the first week. Their eyes and ears are both sealed and non-functioning, although their sense of smell is active. This is the sense that enables them to find their dam and food source.

It is during this period that we will begin skills development; well before the ability to learn; even before their eyes have opened. We will introduce their involuntary systems to changing positions; positions that are not normal for pups this young. We will apply stress in very small amounts and then allow their bodies to adjust. The protocol we will use, the Bio-Sensor, when correctly applied, has been proven to strengthen the immune systems, create stronger heartbeats and promote more rapid recovery to stressful situations in adult dogs. The Bio-Sensor protocol will be explained in great detail in Section Three.

Transitional Period
~ 13 days – 20 days

At approximately two weeks of age, the eyes and ears will begin to open. Although the eyes will not be fully functional until approximately ten weeks of age, some vision is present shortly after the eyes open. The pup can begin to hear as soon as the ear canals begin to open. Usually the pup will have full hearing by the end of this period or the beginning of the Awareness Period.

In an effort to further stimulate the audio and visual segments of the puppies' brains, we need to begin exposing the pups to soft noises and changing visual effects. This is easily accomplished by playing classical music at a lower than normal volume and by having a television on with the volume turned down.   Classical music works well because of the changes in tempo and the shifting from soft stringed instruments to more violent percussion instruments.   The light from the television will offer a variety of visual effects as the lights shift from one scene to the next.   These audio and visual stimuli seem to provide an increase in brain activity as the eyes and ears try to decode the new sights and sounds.

Awareness Period

~ 21 days – 28 days

As this period begins, the sense of hearing should be fully functioning, and vision should continue to improve. This is the time to introduce sudden sounds in a controlled manner, without excess amounts of stress. Furthermore, the environment needs to be kept as stable as possible. The litter should not be moved during this period.

Socialization Period

~ 3 weeks – 14 weeks

Beginning at three weeks and continuing until the litter is about fourteen weeks old, several of the critical periods overlap or have a number of aspects occurring at once. The first part of the Socialization Period, (three – seven weeks) is the best time to socialize the litter to other animals. Other animals may include dogs other than the mother, cats, goats, sheep, etc. This is the traditional time when many livestock guardian breeds are placed with the livestock they will be guarding.

I cannot stress too strongly how much care must be used at this time. If you are going to introduce young puppies to other animals, make sure you know the temperament of the other animals as well as the medical history of these animals. It is, however, extremely important to engage in this socialization. Even with mothers that are protective of the litter, this can be accomplished once you have found animals that are healthy and safe. We will cover this process in Section Three.

Beginning at the fourth week and continuing for eight to ten weeks, the puppies are very open to socialization with people. It is critical that puppies remain with their littermates and dam during this time of socialization. During this period the puppies learn many of their life lessons. This is the perfect opportunity to teach basic skills such as sit, down, stand. It is also an excellent time to begin teaching bite inhibition, which is by far the single most important skill a dog will ever learn. The one event that no owner will be able to overlook is a bite from a dog that causes serious injury to a person. House training should also be well under control before this critical period concludes. Finally, we cannot overlook the social skills. Research indicates that exposing pups to one stranger a day for only ten minutes during this critical period can make a tremendous difference in the social skills of the adult dog. Socialization, bite inhibition, and house training will be discussed in great detail in Section Three.

First Impact Period
~ 8 weeks – 11 weeks

The First Impact Period, often referred to as the "First Fear Period," begins at around eight weeks of age. As noted above, the puppies may not have fully functioning sight until ten weeks of age. The adjustment to the full sight and the confusion that this must cause may be one of the contributing factors to this period's being called a fear period. Many times items that the pup was once comfortable with will produce a reaction similar to the pup's reaction when novel items are introduced.

This is the traditional time when most puppies go to their new homes. As we will discuss in Section Three, there is a better way. So, let's first analyze this common practice. During this very important critical period we remove the puppy from his littermates and familiar environment to a new location to live with strangers. In most instances, these strangers (the puppy's new family) will almost immediately take him to the office of another stranger (their vet) where he will be examined and given shots. To compound matters, if we have let the pup go to the new home at eight weeks old, the puppy may not even have the advantage of full sight! Then, when the dog is an adult, we will wonder why he doesn't like vets or family rides.

If puppies do go to new homes during this period, the breeder must take great care to make sure that the family setting is as secure and non-threatening as possible. The breeder also should be certain that the new family understands how to introduce novel items and situations as well as the importance of making the puppy's new experience pleasant and non-stressful.

Many fearful adult dogs have issues that can be traced back to experiences during this critical period that were traumatic for the puppy not because of the experience itself but because it occurred during this critical developmental period. In most cases, repercussions from these incidents could have been easily prevented had the owner or breeder taken into consideration the puppy's vulnerability at this time.

Seniority Classification Period
~ 13 –16 weeks

At the start of the Seniority Classification Period, many of the puppies have recovered from the First Impact Period, and are beginning to "find" themselves as individuals. In the latter part of this period, teething begins and brings with it several new concerns. Within the next three or four weeks many crucial decisions will be made that may affect the development of the adult temperament.

During this time, the litter, if left together, will usually begin to establish a rank structure. Puppies that have the inclination to be dominant may attempt to dominate the other dogs within the litter. The excessive expression of dominating behavior can contribute to the development of a dog that will later be classified as a bully. It may also inhibit the mental and emotional growth of the more submissive puppies in the litter. For this reason, littermates should have large amounts of time separate from each other. I try to separate them just prior to the beginning of the Seniority Classification Period. I often put them in adjacent outside runs so they can see each other but have the "space" to grow and develop their own personalities free from the influence of their littermates.

A number of other behaviors begin to present at this time. Resource guarding, such as food guarding, chew bone guarding, or toy guarding, may become evident. Biting and rough play may also become more frequent. One reason for this is that teething may have begun.

The breeder must exercise good parenting during this period. Food sharing games as well as beginning bite inhibition will assist with resource guarding and inappropriate biting. We need to establish strong a basic skills history prior to this developmental period. Failure to do so will greatly increase the probability of other behavior problems. Rules should have been established for biting and playing and, most importantly, everything must have been kept very positive! We want to build a strong desire to work; we want to instill a strong bond with people, and we want the dog to have a clear understanding of rules and how to obey them. If we can keep everything we do with the puppy positive and enthusiastic it will aid in the growth of their confidence, demonstrate to them that working as a team is fun and rewarding, and, most importantly, show that the easiest and best way to get what they want is to follow the set rules.

Flight Instinct Period
~ 4 months – 8 months

Many people are confused by the title of this period. This period has nothing to do with the "fight or flight" instinct of a dog. The Flight Instinct Period is when the pups become very brave and investigative. The better socialized they are before this point, the braver and more investigative they will become. That is a very good thing! A puppy that is confident and curious about his environment is less likely to become fearful or phobic as an adult, if we continue to build on the positive.

Many new (and not so new) puppy owners ruin their recalls during this period. The simplest things (like calling a puppy who is obviously focused on investigating new smells, chasing a puppy that doesn't come when called, or punishing him once he does come to you) can crush four months of positive work in one afternoon.

Bad habits such as marking in inappropriate areas can appear at this time. House training should be reinforced, perhaps even re-taught, in order to prevent unwanted territory marking.

Teething is a factor at this age. If pups are left to their own devices, they will sink their teeth into everything you consider valuable and whatever is left within the reach of their jaws. Plenty of Busy Buddies® and Kongs® should be available, (stuffed with tasty treats) not only to protect your possessions, but to instill good, safe chewing habits. One of the most frequently asked questions I have had from clients with a new puppy is "Can you stop them from chewing?" Well, yes, I probably could, but I won't! Puppies need to chew. It is normal, healthy and required during the teething process. It will usually start slacking up around nine months of age, but many dogs will enjoy a good chew toy throughout their life.

Second Impact Period
~ 6 months–15 months

This period is not nearly as well defined as the first impact period. It can last several months but sometimes is over in a few weeks. It may start gradually and build up, but I've seen it happen overnight and end just as quickly. The four-month old puppy who was ready to take on the world may suddenly decide that the whole world is big, bad and out to get him. Many owners make matters worse by forcing the dog to cope with situations about which the dog is apprehensive or by applying corrections when the pup reacts negatively or fearfully to stimuli to which he has been exposed previously. This technique, whereby animals are forced to face their fears (usually in high volumes) in the hope that they will eventually realize that the feared object or situation poses no danger, is known as "flooding." Generally speaking, flooding, as a method of overcoming novel items, even if the pup was once social to the item, is counterproductive and cruel. Reassuring the pup when he appears stressed or frightened, however, appears to be counterproductive as well. The most appropriate response, discussed in detail in Section Three, is to ignore the fearful behavior, encourage investigation of the novel item, and reward positive responses.

Because the Second Impact Period is probably the most misunderstood, and often unexpected, many people mistakenly assume that their new little puppy, who has been doing so well in his skills development, is all of a sudden rebellious, disobedient, hardheaded, and fearful. For this reason it is the most common age for puppies to make the debut into the shelter scene. By continuing to build on the basic skills imprinted by the breeder, we can prevent the pup from this sort of fate. Puppy families must continue to reinforce a positive recall, and not fall into the trap of chasing pups or punishing pups that are slow to come when called. Families must continue to expose the pup to novel stimuli in a positive manner as previously mentioned. This will aid the pup in overcoming the confusion and will prevent fearfulness. How the family handles this lesson may determine, not only how long the puppy remains with this family, but also how the puppy views people for the rest of his life.

Maturity

Temperament and normal adult behavior is usually set by fifteen to eighteen months of age. However, full maturity (mental, emotional and physical) does not occur until around two or three years of age. Not all breeds mature at the same age. Generally, the smaller breeds mature much earlier than the larger breeds. The rate at which dogs mature not only differs from breed to breed but from individual to individual even within the same litter. Each dog's level of maturity must be evaluated on a case-by-case basis.

It is critical that we monitor mature dogs that have cohabitated with others of the same sex. What were once apparent friendships may now turn into challenges for status. If handled carefully and with respect using a positive approach, these friendships can continue without serious conflict.

Households with multiple mature dogs can present problems if the conflicts are not addressed in a timely manner. There are several excellent books that address this situation. My favorite is *Feeling Outnumbered? How to Manage & Enjoy a Multi-dog Household*. It is written by Karen London & Patricia McConnell, and available at Dogwise.com.

DAYS SINCE BIRTH

Neo-natal period
Transitional period
Awareness period

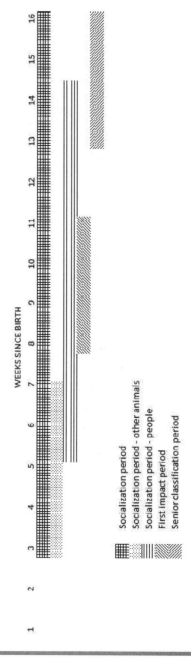

MONTHS SINCE BIRTH

Socialization periods
Flight instinct period
Second impact period

A very pregnant Marilyn
CH Undercover Marilyn Monroe, CGC, RTD

Jessie

The Breeder's Guide to Raising Superstar Dogs

SECTION TWO

Dealing with the Environment

Environmental Factors

The Superstar Program rests on a tripod; each of the three legs are interdependent and essential. The first leg was discussed in the previous section. The Critical Periods tell us "when" to launch the various aspects of the Superstar Program's exercises. The other two legs consist of our recognition of the impact of the environment on the pup and our knowledge of imprinting, the special neurological learning tool that nature has provided.

By definition, the environment includes the circumstances, objects, and conditions by which one is surrounded. And who controls the circumstances, objects and conditions by which the puppy is surrounded from birth to placement with a new owner? The breeder, of course.

Since research has shown that about 35% of a dog's working ability and temperament is inherited; this means that the remaining 65% is the result of his environment. Because he controls the environment, the breeder has the ability to shape an astounding 65% of the temperament and working ability of the puppies he produces. That is an enormous responsibility! This is why I have concentrated the focus of this book on environmental factors.

Traditionally, we tiptoe around the new puppies; we isolate them to provide a quiet place for them to grow; we prohibit people from coming to visit until they reach 8 weeks, 10 weeks, or even 16 weeks.

Although the average age for pups to go to their new families is seven and a half weeks, many breeders allow them to leave their mother as early as four weeks! This is technically a week prior to the pups having the capability to learn. Later in this book we will explore the advantages of retaining the litter for only a few weeks longer than is now considered the average.

The Breeder's Guide to Raising Superstar Dogs

Many breeders do have strict requirements for placement of their pups. Other pups are not so lucky. Regardless of how you advertise, through the internet, newspaper and magazine ads, or a sign in your front yard, you are responsible for the outcome of that puppy. Breeders must accept this as a fact.

Another factor in the environmental influence is the dam. I have often heard breeders say, "She has a great pedigree that contains dogs with super temperaments. She is nervous and a little fearful because of the way she was raised." She might have a great pedigree, and had she been properly raised, she may not have turned out to be nervous and fearful. She may not pass these bad traits to her offspring through genetics. However, the chances are extremely high that these pups will learn from their mother that nervous and fearful behavior is normal. They will learn this during the most impressionable of times, making it as equally imprinted as if it were inherited. If, as a responsible breeder, your program, and the breed in general, requires that this bitch reproduce, her behavior issues should be corrected or controlled prior to the breeding taking place.

If we are to take advantage of the opportunity to influence the majority of the pups behavior and temperament, we have to change our whole way of thinking. This book will go against what some breeders consider normal. It will expose the pups to light, noise, strangers of all species, and to the hustle and bustle of everyday life. Our goal should be to turn this box of coal called a litter into a beautiful setting of highly polished diamonds, which will be our Superstar Dogs!

Imprinting

Konrad Lorenz is considered the "father of imprinting." Lorenz's research, along with that of Oscar Heinroth, indicated that certain behaviors exhibited by animals toward their young were crucial to the survival of their species. These behaviors were "imprinted" on their offspring at specific times, which varied from species to species. In some animals it is a following response; in others it involves the selection of a mate. However, in dogs we can use imprinting to teach many valuable skills that will greatly enhance the quality of life for the dog.

The basic concept of imprinting is familiar to most people. It was popularized more than a decade ago in the movie, *Fly Away Home*. In this movie, a flock of Canadian geese, imprinted on a young girl shortly after they hatched, an followed her ultra-light aircraft on a migratory flight from Canada to a wildlife refuge in the United States. Although the movie version was fictional and romanticized, it was based on the real-life experience of Canadian Bill Lishman, who imprinted his flock of geese on the ultra-light aircraft itself and led them from Ontario to northern Virginia.

Today, imprinting is utilized extensively by horse breeders who touch and handle a foal's entire body within an hour after birth in order to desensitize the foal to human touch and presence. The newborn foal is also exposed to stimuli which in most instances would startle or spook a horse (the sight and sound of flapping plastic or paper for example), but since this is done prior to the activation of the foal's "flight or fight" instinct he tends to accept such stimuli in later life more calmly than a horse which was not imprinted. The end result of the imprinting procedure is a more manageable horse whose training is facilitated.

Even though the concept of imprinting is rather widely recognized today, the tendency of the average person is to identify it with those animals who are imprinted shortly after birth. These animals, the precocial species, become less dependent on their mothers relatively soon after they are born; therefore, the behaviors necessary for survival must be imprinted immediately. For example, a newborn foal in the wild needs to be able to run with and follow his mother if a predator approaches. Included in the precocial species whose imprint behavior has been studied are horses, cows, and geese. The imprint window for these species occurs immediately after birth and is brief.

Fortunately, for those of us who breed dogs, the imprinting window is much wider. Dogs are among the altricial species, those animals that are extremely vulnerable at birth, many of whom cannot see or hear and are completely dependent on the mother for warmth, food, and protection... in short, for survival. Because the altricial offspring remain dependent on the mother for an extended period, the imprint window opens later and remains open longer than the imprint window of the precocial species.

The puppy's imprint window opens at three weeks and remains open through the tenth week. Because of this extended period in which imprinting can occur, many people do not consider this to be true imprinting, but rather an early form of learning. I agree that it is an early form of learning, but it is an intense and concentrated form of learning that is, in effect engraved on the memory plates of their minds. Imprinting is more powerful than teaching an adult dog to sit or speak. This early form of learning can reach the level much of inherited traits; much like the imprinting of a foal or a duckling. Since the similarities tend toward imprinting more than learning, but with a response time much longer than is normal for other species, a more correct term for this type of imprinting might be "social imprinting." However, because this book is geared only to the imprinting of dogs, I will use the simpler term "imprinting."

After a few weeks, the puppies will begin to gain mobility and will soon be venturing away from their mother. As this begins to occur, we can take advantage of their newly developing senses by placing the puppies in situations that force them to use these newfound functions. In some species, the dominant sense involved in imprinting is sight. In other species, sound and smell are also involved. With dogs, the first sense is smell. However, we should treat all senses, sense, sight, sound, touch, and smell, with equal importance.

Imprinting is for life

One of the most important characteristics of imprinting is that the knowledge is retained for life. This fact alone makes the strongest case for structuring the imprinting of puppies during the critical window from three weeks to ten weeks and exploiting this extremely powerful learning opportunity. Imprinting is a fact of the puppy's life. Whether the breeder follows a carefully planned routine or simply allows nature to take its course, the puppy's experiences from week three to week ten will be imprinted. The breeder determines whether what is written on the pages of the puppy's mind will be positive life lessons, negative and/or traumatizing encounters leading to behavior problems, or, very little of anything either positive or negative in the case of a puppy so sheltered and isolated that his life experiences are extremely limited during the imprinting period.

Using the power of imprinting, we can instill a number of important skills at a very early age. Once the pups start to gain mobility and are eating on their own, we can encourage their toilet training in the toilet side of the whelping box and later on, outdoors. We have then established the "norm" for toilet usage. I have included some information on a couple of excellent whelping box designs in the Appendix.

We have to also realize that what gets imprinted is not always what we want to be imprinted. Care must be taken not to allow events or situations to imprint that will set a "norm" causing behavior problems later in life. One of the most common is visits to the veterinarian. Many breeders take the litter to the veterinarian's office at around five weeks old. This is well into the imprinting period noted in several studies. We must, at all costs, ensure that all experiences during this very critical period remain enjoyable and non-threatening for the puppy.

One of the primary lessons taught by Dr. Dunbar is that we must picture every situation the way the dog sees it. In the dog's mind, one of two things will happen in every situation. Either things get better for the dog or things will get worse. Looking at situations with this binary approach will assist us in predicting how the pup will perceive the new experience. If we can't ensure that the pup will consider things getting better for him, we should avoid it. The visit to the veterinarian's office is important and certainly necessary. Hopefully, this will be the first of many yearly checkups.

Therefore, our task becomes how do we make this first visit a good experience for the pup. With the help of educated veterinary staff and a veterinarian with a great bedside manner, the task is much more easily accomplished.

It is not enough for the breeder to have an excellent veterinarian; the breeder must also have a good relationship with the doctor and the entire staff of that clinic. If you have developed this relationship, you can usually bring the entire litter to the clinic for a casual, drop-in well-visit. On the well-visit each pup should be handled, given treats, and allowed to play with the staff. Visiting the examination rooms is also a great idea when possible. On these well-visits, the goal is for the pups to have a positive experience. If you can conduct several of these well-visits prior to the first "real" visit, your pups will be more likely to enjoy trips to the vet, even when invasive procedures must be performed.

Dealing with the Novel Situations

Teaching the dog to deal with novel situations or items is really quite simple. Forcing the dog into the novel situation or suddenly exposing the dog to high levels of the fearful stimulus (also known as "flooding") rarely works and often increases the sensitivity to the fearful stimuli (known as sensitization) and increases the likelihood of more serious problems developing. Additionally, when flooding is used during early developmental periods, there is an increased chance that other problems not directly related to the actual situation may arise. This condition is known as "fallout."

Beginning in the Active Introduction Phase, you will probably observe the puppies startling to unfamiliar stimuli. Novel situations are best dealt with in a very positive manner.

When a puppy or a dog reacts negatively to a novel stimulus, the response of the handler should be calm. The handler should ignore any negative reaction by the dog. Avoid correcting the dog or reassuring the dog with things like "It's OK, boy." Instead, the handler should focus on the novel stimulus. First, the handler should move into close proximity to the stimulus. The handler should then wait a few minutes to give the dog an opportunity to investigate the stimulus on his own accord. If he does, then the handler should give him a tasty treat and praise him.

If he does not investigate the stimulus, we then take it a second step. We shower the stimulus with attention. We gently touch the stimulus and wait for the dog to investigate (Onlookers will view this as proof that you are out of your mind). Be careful not to move or shake the stimulus. If this still does not cause the dog to investigate, we move to step three; we talk to the stimulus. Carry on a conversation with the stimulus acting as though this is a perfectly normal activity. Remember, do not move or shake the stimulus. Something about the stimulus stressed the dog. It was more than likely either the sound or the movement that caused this stress. By our actions, we have encouraged the dog to investigate the stimulus on his own. This builds the pup's confidence, increases his investigative nature, and most importantly, causes little or no negative effect. At any time the dog investigates or shows interest, be quick with a treat and lots of praise. We will cover this in more detail in Section Three.

Am/Can Select CH Gamegards Guns A Blazin', TT, CGC, RTD

SECTION THREE

The "Superstar" Approach to Imprinting

The "Superstar" Approach to Imprinting

The application of the Superstar Dog Program begins on the day the puppies are born. Treat every puppy the same,  regardless of obvious characteristics that would preclude him from competing or participating in certain activities. For instance, if a pup is the wrong color or possesses incorrect markings, continue with the entire routine regardless. If at any time a puppy shows a total disregard for any particular activity, continue to present the activity. You do not want to make a premature decision as to where this puppy's talents lie. Puppies need to be exposed to many different activities and you should note his interest level in each of the activities in which he participates. This information is also extremely useful when it is time to make the decision as to which home he will go.

We are dealing with a domesticated animal that, by definition, "should be" a part of our society;

interacting with man. Far too often, in an effort to protect the puppies, we isolate the litter and make every effort to prevent the type of stimulation that the puppies truly need. We have a relatively short period in which to teach them how to survive in our world. In some species, the window in which this can be accomplished with the greatest ease (the imprinting window), is open for only a few hours after birth. With dogs, we are most fortunate to have nearly three months to accomplish this. Far too often, we waste this excellent opportunity to teach the puppy lessons which will remain with him for a lifetime.

The Passive Introduction Phase
~ Birth - 3 weeks

We have our first chance affect the lives of our litter when the puppies are in the First Critical Period. I have found this to be the most over-looked of these critical periods. To the average person, the pups are just big blobs and do not appear to do anything interesting. However, SO much can be accomplished in the first few days of life.

Bio-Sensor
During this time, the primary concern has always been to keep the pups warm and leave mom to her

duties. However, breeders must realize that we need to assume a larger role during this period. The pups should be handled daily. I suggest the use of a program called Bio-Sensor. Bio-Sensor, commonly called the "Super Dog Routine," consists of five exercises lasting between three to five seconds with each pup, and administered once a day. The U. S. Military used it as part of their breeding program until the program was halted in the 1970s as a cost cutting measure. The dogs produced in this program had an average "working" life of fourteen years? Can you imagine our dogs "working" until they are fourteen years old! After age fourteen, the military dogs were retired to enjoy a well-earned rest.

In essence, the Bio-Sensor exposes the pup to controlled stress. Stress is introduced in small increments; the pup is allowed to recover, and then another stressor is applied. The positive results of the utilization of this program evident in adult dogs exposed to the Bio-Sensor exercises as puppies include faster recovery from stress, an improved immune system, improved heart function, and greatly improved social skills.

The Bio-Sensor routine should begin on the third day after birth. The routine consists of five exercises performed on each puppy, once a day. Complete the entire five-exercise routine with one puppy before moving on to the next puppy. In the beginning each exercise lasts three seconds; after three or four sessions the time for each exercise is increased to four seconds. The four-second exercises continue for four or five days, after which the time is increased to five seconds per exercise for the remainder of the fourteen-day program. It is most important to remember that, while limited neurological stimulation at this age promotes the puppy's development, over-stimulation can have a decidedly negative effect. The puppies should be exposed to the Bio Sensor program only once each day. None of the exercises should ever exceed the maximum time of five seconds, and the program should not continue longer than fourteen days.

The Bio-Sensor exercises are conducted in the whelping box with the mother present. The only equipment required is a cotton-tipped swab, a cold wet towel, two hands and a litter of puppies. With a little practice, you will find the program runs relatively smoothly, taking between fifteen seconds and twenty-five seconds per pup.

Tactile stimulation

While holding a single puppy snugly in one hand, use the Q-tip to stimulate the pup between his toes. You can use the same foot each time or switch between feet. I have found little or no difference. You may or may not see any sort of reaction from the pup while this stimulation is taking place. Begin with the minimum time and increase the time as previously described.

Head up position

Safely hold the pup between your hands with the pup's head held perpendicular to the ground, (straight up), so that its head is directly above its tail. Begin with the minimum time and increase the time as previously described.

Head down position

Use a similar hand technique as used in the "Head Up Position" except the pup is reversed; the head is pointing down and the tail is pointing upwards. Begin with the minimum time and increase the time as previously described.

On the back position

Place the pup with his back in the palm of one hand; place the other on the pup's chest holding firmly. The pup should be facing towards the ceiling. The pup may wiggle, so be prepared with a gentle but firm grip. Begin with the minimum time and increase the time as previously described.

Thermal stimulation

You will need a cold damp cloth (refrigerated for at least five minutes) for this exercise. Place the towel on the floor next to the whelping box. Place the pup on the cloth, feet down. Allow the pup to move around as he wishes. Begin with the minimum time and increase the time as previously described.

As you are completing the Bio-Sensor program, the puppies are entering the Transitional Period. This period is usually obvious in that the pup's eyes open and the ears begin to open. This is an excellent time to introduce stimuli which will not only decrease the likelihood that the pups will become photophobic (the fear of light) or phonophobic (the fear of noise) but will also promote neurological development. We can do this by exposing the litter to low level changing lights, such as a television (with the volume turned down). I am sure everyone has seen the changing light in a room with the lights off and the TV on. The puppy's brain will try to adjust to the different light levels, causing the brain to begin to work earlier than it would in the usual whelping room environment. This is also true with sounds. Use classical music at a low volume to achieve the auditory stimulation. Classical music is performed using many different instruments, which appears to stimulate the brain to try to hear each sound.

The Breeder's Guide to Raising Superstar Dogs

As the litter's activity level increases, Add some novelty to the sight and sounds. Households vary in the number of people and the activity levels. Noise levels also vary. I believe in maintaining the normal activity level within the household. If you have an active and noisy household, adjust the program accordingly. For the average household where you can carry on a conversation in a normal tone of voice, Begin with a small shaker can. Starting with small plastic aspirin bottles with a few washers or pennies securely fastened inside them, begin to shake the bottle as you approach the whelping box and continue shaking the bottle while in the vicinity of the litter. After several days of using the shaker can outside the whelping box, place the shaker can into the whelping box while continuing to rattle the can. This exposes the pups not only to the sight and sounds, but also to novel items. This type of exercise will reduce the chances of the pup becoming neophobic (fear of novel and/or startling stimuli). As the pups become more aware of their surroundings, increase the size of the can and the way you put it into the whelping box. Begin by placing the larger shaker can at the opposite end of the whelping box away from the pups. Progress to tossing the shaker can right near the pups. Once the litter shows some comfort and interest in the shaker can routine, we can begin to make use of the can in a more startling manner. For example, while the pups have cuddled together for a nap, toss the can near the pile of pups. This will prepare the pups for that three-year old child who rudely awakens the sleeping dog.

Remember, we are trying to set the standard for what the puppy considers normal. If you have a noisy household with lots of loud voices, banging of pots and pans, screaming children and the like, this will set the status quo. As a rule, I do not recommend reducing the noise level just for the sake of the puppies. However, if the noise level or the activity level causes stress for the dam, reducing the activity and the noise would be prudent. If this is necessary, hopefully it can be accomplished without relocating the litter, which should be avoided in the early stages except when absolutely necessary.

**Am/Intl Ch. Undercover U. S. M. C. "Uzi" –
Above two weeks old, below two years old.**

The Active Introduction Phase
~ 3 - 4 weeks

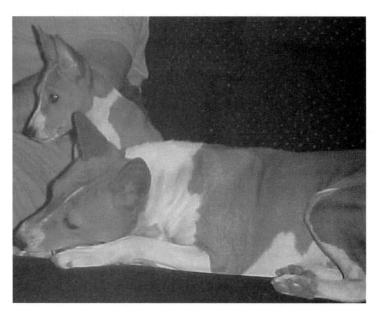

By this time, eyes and ears are open and at least partially functional. The use of shifting lights (TV with the volume tuned down) and soft classical music should be continued to stimulate the functions of the brain. Another idea is to substitute a CD of different sounds for the classical music. Legacy Canine has a wonderful selection; everything from babies crying, household appliances, fireworks, gun shots, and even dogs barking. You can find these online at http://legacycanine.com.

Also during this phase, puppies are usually started on gruel. I use a large coned puppy pan. When I place it with the pups, I tap on it with a wooden spoon creating a "dinner bell" effect. While the pups are eating (or wallowing in the food) make it a point to touch each puppy. Touch around the face and mouth. With some of the gruel on your finger, put the gruel into each pup's mouth. This prepares the pups for the food games, which will come later. It is also helpful to introduce hand feeding at this time. Just spend a few minutes with each puppy individually while they eat and offer some of their gruel from your hand or finger. This creates a positive association with people around the food bowl.

As the activity level of the puppies increases, intensify the use of the shaker cans. As reactions to the shakers become less, you can switch to larger shakers. By this time, the shaker-can should be the size of a small (one pound) coffee can. When beginning with the larger shaker-can, increase the distance from the litter and slowly work towards the whelping box. Do not limit yourself to just shaker cans. Be imaginative. Use as many household noises as possible, following the same procedure. If you started novel noise stimulation as previously outlined, you should be back to the whelping box in just a few sessions. As you move closer to the whelping box, the shaker-can should be shaken with more vigor. If done properly, the pups usually offer one of two reactions; they either totally ignore the shakers or they get very excited anticipating interaction with their human buddies, and possibly some more tasty treats!

It is also helpful to begin drive development at this time. Begin slowly with a small washcloth or dish cloth on a string. Place the cloth in the whelping box or play area near where the puppies are playing. Make the cloth come to life with quick jerking motions, maybe even slowly dragging the cloth over the pups. Once the pups show an interest, allow them to play with it in short sessions. Always let the pups end up with the cloth. Contrary to popular belief, building drive does not increase aggression. The most common causes of aggression are fear, lack of confidence, and lack of control. This program is designed to build confidence, which reduces fear. Basic skills training, which be introduced in the next phase, will solve the control problems.

As noted earlier, socialization to other animals should begin in this phase. It is the responsibility of the breeder to make sure that the animals that will be used to socialize the puppies are healthy and that the young pups will be safe around them. The first introduction should be a short sniff session. Once you are sure everyone is okay with each other, longer sessions may be allowed. It is good to socialize the pups to male dogs (at this point they probably have seen only their mother), as well as other females and other breeds. If other species of animals (remember, healthy and safe) are available, then they may be introduced. Many bitches will not allow strange animals around their litter. If this is mom's attitude, wait for her to take a break to stretch her legs and bring another animal in while she is out of the room. Make sure you control mom's access back to the litter to prevent an unexpected return. Even protective moms will usually allow some visitors after a few weeks.

As soon as the pups are walking around on sturdy legs, it is time to begin imprinting the recall. This is best started by clapping your hands and calling the familiar high-pitched, "Pup pup pup pup." When they make their way to you, they should always receive a pleasant welcome. A spot of peanut butter and a good scratch on the head will ensure many happy returns. This must be continued through every phase so that you can be certain a strong recall is in place before the pups advance into the Flight Instinct Period at around sixteen weeks.

The final new experience to which the puppies are exposed in this phase is the expansion of their environment to the out of doors. I usually take my pups outside when they are about four weeks old, carrying the entire litter out for short sessions in the yard. Shortly after their introduction to the yard, begin taking pups outside several times a day to begin their house training. Following a specific schedule will make house training a much easier task for both you and the pups. As a general rule, potty breaks should occur after every meal, after every play session, and when the pups first wake up in the morning or from a nap. This practice should be continued throughout the imprinting phases.

The Skills Phase
~ 5 – 7 weeks

During the Skills Phase, we will begin to imprint some of the basic performance activities including obedience, agility, tracking, and retrieving. Supervised socialization with animals will continue, but we will also begin to focus on socialization to people. The term "well-socialized" is often misused. Some breeders who advertise "well-socialized" or "family-raised" puppies are under the mistaken impression that adequate socialization has been provided by the fact that the puppies have always been around family members. Socialization, as described by Random House Unabridged Dictionary, is:

"A continuing process whereby an individual acquires a personal identity and learns the norms, values, behavior, and social skills appropriate to his or her social position."

This definition tells us a great deal about what must take place to fully socialize our canine friends. If we limit our socialization to family members only, then we have a litter of puppies that is socialized to our family alone. We have limited their exposure to social settings to our home, thereby neglecting the development of skills needed to survive in other types of situations. Failure to provide proper socialization within the prescribed timeframe may result in a dog that his development has been socially retarded.

It is the breeder's job to expose the puppy to a wide variety of experiences and situations to maximize the development of his social skills. This includes meeting as many strangers as possible. It is often said, that the *magic* number associated with puppy socialization is one hundred strangers by the time he is fourteen weeks old. Regardless, one hundred is certainly a great goal. Scott and Fuller research shows that if a puppy has not seen a stranger before seven weeks of age, he is not likely to approach strangers without encouragement. After fourteen weeks of age with no exposure, he may never approach a stranger.

The breeder can get things off to a positive start by getting as many people to visit the pups as possible. If we use the number one hundred as our goal, we need a little over eleven visitors a week. Some may be visitors in the home; others will be encountered in settings outside the home. As to who the visitors are, well, be creative! Make sure you cover a number of types, including men, women, children, elderly people, young people, hyper people, calm people, loud people, smokers, non-smokers, different races, people with hats, sunglasses, people with facial hair, Halloween masks, people with walking canes or walking frames, and anything else that comes to mind. Use your imagination! Everything to which you introduce you puppy is one less thing that can cause a problem in the future, provided the introductions are kept positive.

Not all of this has to be accomplished in the fifth week; it should be spread over the next nine weeks. Part of the responsibility of the breeder is to inform the new owners as to which stage of the socialization process the puppy has completed, and to make sure that that they are fully instructed as to how to carry on with the process. Always remember that one of the most important phrases in the definition of socialization is "a continuing process." **Socialization continues throughout the dog's life**. I have yet to see a dog that is too social!

When the Skills Phase begins at five weeks, the puppies' brains are capable of learning in the more traditional sense.   Lights and music were used during the Transitional Period to increase brain activity. For this reason, imprinting will be more productive and more fun for both the breeder and the puppies.   At this point, skills sessions should be brief, only one or two minutes per puppy. Although multiple sessions can be done in a day, I recommend that the number of one-on-one sessions be limited to only a couple per day for the first two or three weeks.   After every pup has had a chance to catch on to what we are trying to accomplish, I like to have several "group" sessions with the entire litter.

Work with the pups one-on-one. Conduct the basic skills and handling exercises on an elevated surface such as a small grooming table or coffee table. This prevents the breeder from working in an uncomfortable position and it limits the size of the pup's world, helping him to focus his attention on the breeder. Begin by using a treat, such as peanut butter, to lure the puppy into the three basic positions; sit, down, and stand. Teaching all three positions at once may seem like a lot, but they do these activities many times every day without your help. Although I don't associate a verbal command with the action until much later, I do use consistent hand signals right from the start.

While the pup is focused on the lure, you have an excellent opportunity to teach him that it's okay to be touched. Rub the pup all over his head and his back, touching the paws and picking them up is a positive way to show the pup that people touching his body is a good thing. Remember to teach the "3-Ts," that is, teeth, toenails and testicles. Even if they do not have the testicles, it is a good idea to practice touching in that area, just to get them used to it.

To teach the first "T," the teeth, start by touching the lip and giving a treat. Once the puppy is okay with that, raise the lip and give a treat. Continue until opening the mouth is a fun thing for both you and the puppy, and he is more than willing to have you admire his teeth.

The second "T," the toenails, will require the use of a similar approach. Begin by touching each foot and giving a treat. Then pick the foot up and give a treat. Once the pup is comfortable with the feet being touched and picked up, begin to play with the toenails, one by one, and give a treat. Continue with this process until you can spend a few seconds with each toenail, with little or no reaction from the pup. Once the pup is comfortable in this situation, you can then begin to clip each nail, and of course, give a treat as you finish each nail. If a grinder will be used to do nails, it is a good idea to have the grinder running at low speed while you are playing with the nails just so the noise is not new the first time you use the grinder. When the time comes to use the grinder, a quick, light touch of the nails with the grinder is a good start. Do not expect to get the nails correctly trimmed on the first attempt. Remember, we are imprinting; we want the pup to learn that nail trimming is a normal activity that he should accept quietly and without a fuss. We do not want him to associate it with a wrestling match.

The third "T" is testicles. This is usually the easiest task to accomplish if started early. However, I know many people have been bitten for touching or even reaching for a dog's testicles. This exercise needs to be performed with the female pups as well. They too will need to be examined at some point. If the dogs are going to be shown in conformation, they will definitely be examined. You can begin this exercise by touching the dog at the base of the tail (or where the tail should be) and giving a treat. Then rub the base of the tail and give a treat. Next, touch the tail and you guessed it, give a treat. Once the pup is fully comfortable with this, or when you touch the rear end, he looks for the treat, you can then move on to touch between the rear legs. First, just a touch and a treat, then a touch, pause, give a treat, then a touch hold, give a treat, and finally, a touch, a squeeze, and then a treat.

While teaching the three "T's," should you encounter resistance from a pup, remember not to force the pup. Switch to a different treat, such as cheese, chicken or liver. Watch the pup's reaction as you begin the exercise. When you reach a point where the pup first starts to get uncomfortable, stop. Use that point as an intermediate goal. Once the pup is comfortable with that point, then progress a little closer to the target area. Continue this until you can touch the teeth, toenails, and testicles with little or no reaction from the pup.

Since we have mentioned conformation and outlined the procedure for preparing the dog to be examined, this might be a good time to address the issue of whether a prospective conformation dog should be taught to sit. It is a common misconception that if a dog sits in the conformation ring it will hurt his chances of winning. There is so much wrong with this concept that I hardly know where to begin to try to correct it. I will start by saying that as a conformation judge, I have never penalized a dog for sitting unless it prohibited my ability to evaluate the dog. As I stated previously, we are not TEACHING the dog to sit; he does this hundreds of times each day, all on his own. He would be too tired to be a show dog if he never sat or lay down. All we are doing is associating a word with an action the puppy is already performing. Placing the same importance on all three positions lessens the chances of an inappropriate sit. *Should* the dog sit, a simple cue to the appropriate position should correct the situation, which, as a judge would impress me, displaying that the dog does have a brain as well as correct conformation. Finally, if the dog is truly incapable of learning to sit and still be a competitive show dog, maybe we have placed too much emphasis on the "show" and not enough on the "dog." In the thirty-plus years that I have been involved with dogs and dog shows, I cannot tell you how many times I have run from the conformation ring to the obedience ring and vice-versa and never once can I remember a dog sitting or standing out of context.

The next activity we will imprint is the use of the dog nose. The remarkable ability to use his sense of smell is probably the most misunderstood of all canine attributes. The puppy uses his sense of smell to find his mother only seconds after he enters this world. Once this sense is fully developed, not only does it serve the dog's purposes, but we can use it to make our life better. When we smell a pot of vegetable soup cooking on the stove, we say, "Wow, that soup smells really good." When our dog smells that same soup, he says, "Those carrots smell really good and the onions were fresh out of the garden and ..." The olfactory system of the canine is used to detect bombs and drugs that no machine and certainly no human would ever discover. The dog is used to sense medical conditions giving his owner plenty of time to prepare for an upcoming medical attack; and we even use the canine's powerful sense of smell to alert us to cancerous tissue, many times months before medical science has a clue to its presence.

The Skills Phase is the perfect time to encourage the puppy to use his sense of smell in tracking exercises. There are two popular ways to begin basic tracking imprinting. One popular method is to place a small treat on the ground a short distance from the pup. Point to the ground and slowly move your finger toward the cookie. Once the pup reaches the treat, allow him to eat the treat and add enthusiastic verbal praise. Another popular method, and my favorite, (although I've used both with success) is to encourage the pup to "go find someone." This is done by one person lightly restraining the pup while another person plays with the pup and then runs a short distance and out of sight, such as around a corner, while still calling the pup. After a brief period, the restrainer releases the pup. If the pup does not run to find the hiding person, the restrainer runs and finds the person. When the pup joins in, he is rewarded with a little play session or a treat. When the pup's desire to find the hiding person increases, it is time to add a verbal cue such as, "Go find Mommy," or "Go find Mary." During the first week of tracking imprinting, keep the distances short and do only two or three hides each session. It is a good idea to switch the tracklayer (which, to this point has probably been the breeder) and the restrainer so the pup learns to "go find" more than one person.

The Skills Phase is a good time to introduce other novel items. Start with simple things like an unopened umbrella sitting in a corner. Once the pups seem comfortable with that, in the next session, place it in the  middle of the play area. Next, partially open the umbrella in the corner of the play area, and then systematically, over a number of sessions, move the partially opened umbrella towards the center of the play area. This is followed by repeating the same sequence with an umbrella that has been fully opened prior to the pups entering the play area. Finally, with the pups playing in the area, open the umbrella in the corner of the play area, then, once everyone is comfortable with the umbrella being opened at a distance, move the openings progressively closer until the umbrella can be opened in the middle of the room with the puppies all around and experiencing no discomfort. Use your imagination to come up with other novel items and follow a similar sequence of events for handling the introduction of each item.

You may encounter a situation where most of the litter is doing well with a novel stimulus, but one or two pups still have problems with it. I would encourage working with the stimulus with the pups during their one-on-one time. I have found it to be effective to place the stimulus in question near the area where you are playing or conducting your one-on-one skills exercises. Conduct the exercise as you normally would, paying little or no attention to the stimulus. As the sessions progress, move the stimulus closer and closer to the working area. Before you know it, the pup will openly accept the stimulus. It is important to "teach" the pup how to accept novel items as early in life as possible. Doing so will enable the pup to more quickly accept other novel stimuli later in life with a minimal amount of stress.

If you have not taken your pups to different locations, the Skills Phase is a good time to begin to get them out. My house is surrounded by three training fields where hundreds of dogs visit on a weekly basis. There is no place on my property where other dogs have not been. I personally take my pups onto the training fields at four weeks of age. However, you should consult your veterinarian prior to taking your pups to areas where they may be exposed to diseases. Many people with whom I train with are also breeders who take advantage of the opportunity to expose their puppies (four weeks and older) to the smells, sights, and sounds of a training field. Most of these breeders bring their pups out once or twice a week for socialization to people, dogs, and a visit to a novel location. An exercise pen set up near the field is a great way to accomplish this.

If you chose to begin building drive in the Active Introduction Phase, this should be continued and intensified. By now, you probably need to start using a "flirt pole," a flexible rod with a string attached at the top and a cloth attached to the other end to the string. This allows you to make quicker movements with the cloth or "rag" (hence the name, "rag work"). A commercial version of the flirt pole, called "Chase-N-Pull Toy" is available at www.dogwise.com, or you can substitute a sturdy fishing pole. A few minutes a couple of times a week is usually enough; however, many people perform it daily. You can also do the rag work with the litter as a whole. Rag work is quite commonly used by trainers who train for protection sports, lure coursing, and other activities where high prey drive is desired. The moving of the rag encourages the development of prey drive; catching the rag and the shaking of the rag afterwards build confidence. If you have developed good control through skills exercises while building prey drive, you have actually decreased the likelihood of a puppy using his prey drive in an inappropriate manner. This, along with proper socialization and the all-important bite inhibition, will make the puppy even less likely to engage in negative exercises of prey drive.

At six weeks the imprinting we started at five weeks is continued. With the basic skills, we can phase out the peanut butter and switch to another treat such as string cheese or another small tidbit type treat of high value. It is helpful to always have treats of different "value" with you. For instance, use a small piece of kibble for routine exercise. When the pup does the exercise exceptionally well or accomplishes a task for the first time, use a treat of higher value, such as a piece of string cheese or a bite of liver or chicken.

We should begin to start phasing out the "lure" and replacing it with a timely "reward." The pup should now be ready for you to apply a verbal cue to the positions. The use of hand signals will probably still be required for another week or so. The proper procedure would look like this: you give the verbal cue, allow the pup a second to respond. If he does, give a reward; if he does not respond immediately, follow up with the hand signal, then give the reward once the task is accomplished.

During the second week of the Skills Phase, tracking should continue. While the distances of the tracks should increase slightly, the encouragement used to assist the pup in seeking should be reduced.

Agility imprinting can also begin during this same phase. Now, before you jump the gun, no, I am not going to have six-week puppies doing withers-height jumps. We will begin agility imprinting with a dowel rod, a broom handle, or the bar jump pole lying flat on the ground. Begin to play with the pup near the dowel, and as the pup starts to cross over the dowel, offer verbal praise. Once the pup has the general idea, continue the same drills except move the dowel closer to the actual jump uprights. If your obstacles allow for a zero jump height, place the dowel rod on the ground between the jump uprights and continue the drills. Teaching the pup to actually negotiate obstacles is not the real objective here. Exposing the pup to the equipment and instilling confidence in the agility arena environment is the primary goal at this point.

The "Ball on the Wall" game, which is utilized to imprint retrieving skills, can be introduced during the Skills Phase. Some pups will not begin to actively participate until later in the phase, but I usually introduce it near the beginning of this phase in order to obtain a reading on the pups' progress in the development of prey drive. However, the primary purpose of the ball on the wall game is to imprint retrieving.

You play the game by sitting on the floor with your legs spread wide apart and the bottoms of your feet touching the wall in front of you. With the pup in the apex of your legs, get the attention of the pup with a tennis ball (depending on the breed, a smaller ball may be needed). Once you have the pup's attention, toss the ball against the wall. The objective is to have the pup chase the ball, but not actually catch the ball until it is on the way back to you. So, the ball is thrown, the pup chases it. The ball hits the wall and is returning to you when the pup catches up to it. Now the pup has the ball and is headed back toward you. Isn't this what we want in a retrieve? Without thinking about the situation, the pup is being imprinted to bring the object back to you. Sometime the pups may show little or no interest when the ball game is introduced. Repeat the exercise daily and try to develop interest. Although some pups may never play the game completely, I have Basenjis who are as ball crazy as Malinois, all because of early introduction and persistence!

When the pup returns with the ball, avoid taking the ball away  from the puppy. Instead of taking the ball, present another ball and when he drops the ball he is carrying, toss the one you are holding. This enables you to avoid any conflict over the first ball. If he finds the first ball so interesting that he doesn't want to release it, do everything you can to make YOUR ball more interesting, even to the point of tossing it against the wall and getting it yourself. Avoiding conflict is a very important rule in this game.

Don't forget to continue socializing with supervision. Keep a record count of how many people each pup has been in contact with and how many different locations the pups have visited. Pups should continue to be exposed to novel items. This will test your ability to be creative! Continue your rag work to build drive.

Although resource guarding normally does not usually present itself until after the twelfth week, it may begin to manifest much earlier. In an effort to curb this behavior, I start food drills at around six weeks. After all, you are never too young to have good manners. As we have previously discussed, this is easily started by placing your hand in the food bowl while the litter is eating and offering extra little goodies while your hand is around their mouth. While working one-on-one with the pups, you can offer the pup dry food or if you use a dry food formula for your gruel, you can hand feed that.

At seven weeks, the drills you've been conducting should continue. Each puppy should have an opportunity to do all of the skills exercises at least once a day. In the one-on-one sessions, the pups should be responding to the hand signal and many will begin to respond to the verbal signal.

In the Ball on the Wall game, the tossing distance can increase so that your feet are a short distance from the wall. As the pup progresses and freely returns the ball to you, increase the distance even more.

When tracking, remember to keep all the tracks simple. When the pup catches on to the game, you can increase the level of difficulty in the track by slightly increasing the distance or by providing less assistance from the tracklayer. At the first sign of trouble, offer whatever assistance is needed to make the puppy successful. Calling out to the puppy, or making a distinct noise will usually do the trick. Don't try to progress too rapidly; distance will come with maturity and experience.

During the seventh week, introduce the pups to bodies of water. Begin with a very shallow wading pool. While the pup is engaged in chasing a ball, toss the ball closer and closer to the pool. When the dog seems comfortable, toss the ball into the pool. Most of the time, the water will not deter the pup from getting the ball. On the rare occasion that the pup is hesitant, encourage the pup verbally and if necessary, move the ball closer to the side of the pool to allow the pup to retrieve the ball without entering the pool. Over a period of sessions, move the ball farther from the side of the pool. Before long, the pup will be readily running into the water for the ball.

Two new and very significant concepts are introduced toward the middle or the end of the seventh week. The first, bite inhibition, has by far the most important impact on the survival of your dog. Bite inhibition is the dog's ability to control the proper use of his teeth and the jaws that contain those teeth. Most adult dogs possess forty-two large, dangerous teeth controlled by two very powerful jaws. All dogs are capable of inflicting very serious and even fatal injuries. It is our responsibility as breeders to get this under control at an early age. A bite from a seven-week-old puppy might be a little painful, but it is unlikely you will require medical treatment. However, left unchecked, in six months the results may be much more serious. In his book, *After You Get Your Puppy*, Dr. Ian Dunbar comments,

> "Good bite inhibition does not mean that your dog will never snap, lunge, nip or bite. Good bite inhibition means that *should* the dog snap and lunge, his teeth will seldom make skin contact, and should the dog's teeth ever make skin contact, the inhibited 'bite' will cause little if any, damage."

If bite inhibition is not properly in place by four and a half months, the task becomes increasingly difficult, so difficult that all too often the owner will not spend the time, the effort, or the money to accomplish it. It is imperative that the breeder take advantage of the opportunity to imprint the most basic of all the social skills the dog will ever learn; the one skill that, if lacking, may one day surely cost him his freedom, and perhaps his life. If a puppy fails to sit, his actions, or lack thereof, may put him in harm's way, but seldom does it endanger anyone else. If he bites someone, a human is at risk, which certainly puts the dog at risk along with the owner's personal assets.

Many breeders who breed for protection sports are concerned about how teaching bite inhibition will affect the dog's attitude toward this type of work. I can say with certainty that teaching bite inhibition has no negative effect on a dog competing in protection sports. I do encourage lots of rag work and plenty of tug work for all dogs, especially those intended for protection sports.

Puppies need to bite, and we actually need them to bite. Without this "puppy biting", we would not be able to teach bite inhibition. We start by allowing or even encouraging the puppies to bite our hands. We allow this to continue until the puppy begins to bite overly hard. At that point, we cry out loudly and leave the pup alone. After a short break, (a few seconds) we return and encourage the biting again. Each time the pup bites hard, we cry out and leave the pup alone. When the hard bites occur less frequently, we change the criteria. Instead of crying only on the hard bites, we cry on medium hard bites. Next, we begin to cry out on low-medium bites and so on. Over a period of a few weeks, we will have instilled in the puppy a sense of just how fragile we humans are. They will be convinced that care must be taken when playing with us or we will get hurt and stop playing with them. By the time the puppies are ready to go to their new homes, bite inhibition will be established. The new family only has to continue the work you have begun. In my opinion, the best resource for new families is Dr. Dunbar's *After You Get Your Puppy*. In this book, Dr. Dunbar covers bite inhibition extremely well. It is number one on my referral-reading list for all puppy families regardless of whether they have just acquired their first puppy or they have had a number of puppies in the past.

By this time, the pups have some knowledge of the basic control skills, so we can put this knowledge to practical use. We will introduce the game of "tug of war," which is a great game to teach all pups. It teaches control and patience, it builds confidence, and it reinforces your work with bite inhibition. There are three rules that MUST be enforced from the very beginning of the game:

1. **Only you can initiate the game.**
   I have one "special" tug or toy that is used only for this game. Once the game is over, the tug is put away, out of the pup's reach.

2. **No biting you or your clothes.**
   This will continue along with where you are in teaching bite inhibition. In the early stages, you may allow an accidental touch of your hands or your clothes, but later on, you must react to even a slight brush of your hand by teeth.

3. **When you stop the game, it's over.**
   It's just that simple; when you say "game over," the game is over and the toy is put away.

The puppies are now nearing eight weeks of age. This is your last week to imprint social behavior with other animals. So if you've not done this, now is the time to do so. Continue socializing with people. Check your count and see how close you are getting to the magic number. Don't forget to be as diverse as you possibly can.

Finally, many breeders are beginning vaccinations during this period. Regardless of when you begin vaccinations, or even if you give the pup's vaccinations yourself, pups should make a visit to the veterinarian's office prior to the visit when shots will be given. The process for a successful veterinary visit was addressed in the previous section.

The Final Imprinting Phase
~ 8 – 10 weeks

When the puppies are eight weeks old, they are entering the Final Imprinting Phase. Unfortunately, puppies are usually allowed to go to their new families when they are eight weeks old. I believe that we do the new families and certainly our puppies a disservice when we allow the puppies to leave prior to our completing the imprinting program. Furthermore, as noted in the discussion of critical periods, at eight weeks the puppy is particularly vulnerable because he is beginning the First Impact Period (often referred to as the First

Fear Period). These two factors have led me to conclude that, if at all possible, the puppy should remain in his familiar environment until he is at least ten weeks old and preferably twelve weeks old. If the breeder retains the pups until they are at least ten weeks old, he will have a better idea as to what the pups will be like as adults. This will help him to place the puppies in the most appropriate home environment and to make a better match between each puppy and their new family.

By the time we reach the Final Imprinting Phase you should be relying on verbal commands for all three of the position exercises; sit, down, and stand. The pups should be performing the positions in random order, with speed and enthusiasm and with limited use of treats. We are now ready to take our skills "training on the road," as Brenda Aloff suggests in her book, *Positive Reinforcement, Training Dogs in the Real World.* The training should take place in a number of different locations and on different surfaces; inside, outside, on the grass, on the pavement, and any other place where you can find a suitable spot.

Tracking can also move to the outdoors. An area with relatively short grass works best. Taller grass, as well as areas with little or no grass, presents more of a challenge than pups are ready to encounter at this time. A freshly mowed pasture works really well. Find an open area with only a few trees or some small source of cover. Have the assistant hold the dog's leash while you run a few yards away towards the cover. Just before ducking behind the cover, call your dog and have the assistant run toward you with the dog. A few feet from the cover where you are hiding, have the assistant drop the leash so that the dog finds you without the assistant in tow. When the dog reaches you, make sure to throw him a party. Lavish praise, toys, and treats on him. After a couple of successful "run-a-ways," begin to increase the distance. Then, once the pup has gained some confidence and is finding the track-layer (usually the breeder) without hesitation or stopping to smell the flowers, reduce the length of the track to the distance used when you began outside run-a-ways. Leave an article of clothing that has your scent (such as a hat) at the beginning of the track. Have the assistant turn the puppy so that the pup is looking away from the track while you perform a run-a-way. Once the tracklayer is in position, have the assistant bring the pup back to the starting marker and give the cue to find the tracklayer. If the pup begins to search, the assistant just follows along and lets the pup track. If the pup gets off track, the assistant should remain as close to the track as possible and let the pup attempt to figure it out. The tracklayer can give assistance as needed by simply calling the pup's name. When the pups can track and find the tracklayer with accuracy and confidence, increase the distance.

At eight weeks, I raise the bar in agility...literally. If your agility jumps allow for very low adjustments, (never higher than the pups' elbow) then start doing some easy jumps. Begin by walking over the jump and encourage the pup to come with you. Once the pup is going over the jump with little or no encouragement, add a cue just before the pup starts over the obstacle.

Up to this point, everything we've done with the pups has been off leash, except for tracking. It is a good idea to wait to begin actual leash training near the end of the next phase, the Guiding Phase; however, we can prepare the pups for leash training in this phase. We do this by allowing them to play during their one-on-one sessions while dragging a short string attached to their collars.

Ignore the existence of the string when you conduct your sits, downs, and stands.

A "follow me" cue can also begin early in this phase. Depending upon the size of the litter, and how much time has been spent with each pup, this cue may sometimes be introduced during the previous phase. Using a treat/toy as a lure, begin to move forward. Encourage the pup to follow by your side. We are not attempting to accomplish a true heel here, although I have seen eight-week-old pups who could execute a correct heel after only a few sessions. I work the pups on both right and left sides, using different cues for each side. Initially, the pup should be rewarded for moving forward with you. Once some consistency has been established, begin to require a sit on the stops if you want to imprint an automatic sit.

The "Two-Toy Game" is a great way to improve retrieval skills. The two-toy game is so named because the handler uses two identical motivators (toys, balls, tugs, etc...) to play the game. The technique is similar to that used in the ball on the wall game; one toy is used as a retrieval item and the other is used to entice the pup to come back to us to continue playing. When the pup brings the motivator back, the handler throws the other motivator and recovers the one just released by the pup. It is best to keep this game short in the beginning so that the puppy will not get bored.

Another game that is useful during this phase is the "two-handler" game. The two-handler game, a variation of the tug of war game, can be used to teach the "out" command and will prevent possessiveness of retrieval items later in life. The game teaches the pup that it's okay to give up something that he has worked for, because something better may at hand. Both handlers have toys/tugs. One handler engages the pup in a game of tug, but after a brief session (approximately 15 seconds), the handler freezes and stops the game with the pup. At that exact moment, the other handler moves near the pup's head and begins to tease him with the other tug. When the pup releases the first tug, the second handler engages the pup in an enthusiastic game of tug for a brief period. After a short session (again, approximately 15 seconds), the second handler freezes as the first handler again engages the pup. The sequence repeats for several rotations. Once the pup gets the idea that when the tug freezes there is a more active one nearby, it is time to add a cue. The timing of the cue is important. The cue should be given just before the handler freezes. We want the cue (out) to mean that this game is about to be over, but there is a better game nearby.

This type of "out" training is an excellent developmental skill, regardless of whether the pup is bred for protection sports or not. If the pup is bred for protection sports, now is the time to take the "out" to the next step. When the pup becomes familiar with the concept of the game, the handlers can increase the distance between them and begin to position themselves in places other than at the head of the pup. Anytime the pup appears to be confused, returning to the head position is all that is usually required to correct the situation. The goal is to get the pup to "out" and look to the other handler for a better game. The other handler can give a fight with a tug, or a toss of a tennis ball once the pup heads toward him.

By this time, the basic skills should be coming along nicely. Other exercises can be added when you think the pups are ready. If time permits, and all is going well, I will add a "wait" command, a "leave-it" command, a "get back" command, and a "go to your place/bed" command. The puppies are probably going to their new families at the end of this phase, so anything that you can teach them which may facilitate their transition and adjustment to life with their new family is advantageous for all concerned parties: the puppy, the new family, and you. Having a pup returned by a family who couldn't handle him is never a good situation. You face not only the task of resolving the problems which precipitated his return, but possibly other problems which may have developed since the pup left your house.

If the pups are going to their new families at the tenth week, this may also be your last opportunity for socialization. Take the pups to as many different places as possible. While you are at these new places, don't forget to work on your skills exercises. Remember, dogs do not generalize well. This means that once a cue is learned under certain conditions or at specific locations, that cue might not mean the same thing to the dog in a different environment. Therefore, you may need to re-train some of the exercises. This is normal and can occur at all ages. Be patient! Take a deep breath and move at the pup's pace. Usually in one or two attempts, he will be back on course.

A final note about this phase; the pups should have play sessions together, but some supervision may be required to prevent the more forward pups from bullying the others. The pups will also need time alone. If you have not introduced them to crates, now is a good time. Single-crating works best. This allows the pups to develop their personalities as individuals rather than simply as members of the litter. It also prevents any codependencies from developing. A codependent relationship occurs when multiple dogs rely on each other, often inappropriately. This will be exhibited by the needy dog always looking to the other dogs before making any decision. If separated, such dogs may exhibit signs of stress, sometimes severe, and they may become very vocal. Codependencies in dogs usually occur when littermates are left together beyond twelve weeks. Allowing them to stay together often inhibits their individual psychological growth.

The Guiding Phase
~ 11 – 16 weeks

This is my favorite phase. Whenever possible, I like to keep the pups until they are twelve weeks old. One of the reasons is that I can teach rough play. If I teach the pups how to play rough, then it is very simple to teach them when rough play is inappropriate. If I can have two more weeks of structured socialization, it is highly unlikely that the new families will have a problem with socialization.

Rough play is usually not hard to elicit from pups, especially if you have been doing everything we have covered so far. Grabbing at their feet or gently pushing them away from you is usually enough to bring them back at you with all they have. Continue to rev them up until they are on the verge of being out of control; it won't take long. Then change your demeanor; become very calm. More than likely, the pups will continue to be at full speed. Get their attention and cue them to sit or to lie down. Once they are calm, rev them up again. As the game goes on, increase the frequency of the calm sessions and then the duration of the calm sessions. After they understand the concept, you can conduct obedience skills exercises during the calm sessions.

The most important exercise to concentrate on in this phase is the recall. The Flight Instinct Period starts near the end of this phase or the beginning of the next phase. We began imprinting the recall at about four weeks old, so the pups should have a pretty solid recall at eleven weeks. If recalls are not solid prior to the pup's entering the flight instinct period, you will certainly have problems.

All the other exercises should be continued, increasing time and/or distances as appropriate. It is also helpful to begin some of the more difficult tasks by training in "threes." Training in threes is a simple process that builds confidence and pushes the dog to reach for higher goals. We perform each exercise three times. The first time we ask the pup to perform at his average level of accomplishment in the exercise. We make the next attempt slightly more challenging than the first attempt. The last attempt is a very simple task, even less challenging than the first.

For instance, if a pup has been tracking fifty feet, then that would the first of the threes. The next track would be somewhat more challenging, let's say sixty feet. It is important not to make the second leg so difficult that the pup can't successfully complete it. The handler must be ready to assist the pup so that he does not fail. The final track would be somewhat less than the first track, say twenty-five or thirty feet. This last leg serves as a motivator for the dog. In his mind, he just completed a really difficult exercise. Following that with a simple task increases the significance of the accomplishment of the second leg in the dog's mind. Just when he was questioning his abilities because of the level of difficulty of the second leg, he then makes another attempt and finds that the exercise was not as difficult as he remembers. This process works well for pups and adults.

The last task during this imprinting phase is finalizing the social imprinting. This by no means implies that all socialization will have been completed. Since the puppy's imprinting phases are ending, socialization beyond this stage will not be imprinted. As stated previously, socialization is continuous. However, if the steps outlined in the imprinting phases of this books have been followed, future socialization can be easily accomplished.

It is my recommendation that pups stay with their breeder until they are twelve weeks old. This enables the breeder to supervise the socialization of each pup, to ensure the pups are properly imprinted with life skills, and the inoculations are nearly completed. This greatly reduces the likelihood of common behavior problems developing. The fewer behavior problems the puppy has, the easier the transition from the breeder to the new puppy home.

Sometimes keeping pups until they have reached twelve weeks old is not possible. If this is the case, then I strongly advise against placing pups prior to ten weeks. This is just a couple of weeks longer than the current average. It should be clear to everyone that the "average" is not working for us now.

The Training Phase
~ 4 months – 1 year

By the time the dog reaches this phase he is, hopefully, living with the family with whom he will spend many long and happy years. If the breeder properly imprinted the puppy, training beyond this point should go smoothly.

I encourage all owners and trainers to use this time in the young dog's life to promote a positive relationship and to build bonds. This can be accomplished with motivational training and fun games that require the dog to think and to be in control of his actions. It is possible to have lots of fun, allowing the pup to be a puppy, yet still maintain the level of obedience and control previously established. It is essential to build on imprinted skills and to work on perfecting household manners and social skills. However, I prefer not to introduce formal training or competition training until the dog is around twelve months old.

There are several excellent books on training puppies at this age. I suggest that breeders provide a list of books as well as the names of local trainers the breeder considers to be competent and respected. Recently, a breeder who lives on the other side of the country contacted me. She was placing a dog near my home and was interviewing trainers to recommend to her puppy's new family. She was doing the same with veterinarians. I thought, "What a wonderful idea!" To go to the trouble of researching trainers and veterinarians in a far off city is one of the signs of a caring, responsible breeder. Some excellent sources for locating trainers nationwide are listed in the Appendix. I suggest you find several trainers in the area where your pup will reside and call to interview each one prior to suggesting them to your pup's family, especially if this is a first-time home.

SECTION FOUR

Housekeeping

Selecting the Right Home

Every breeder's goal should be to produce a well-rounded pup who will be a valued member of a selected family for many years. No breeder thinks, "This pup may end up in a shelter with behavior problems that I might have prevented." However, even if the breeder has faithfully followed the program described in the preceding pages, this is only the first part of the formula for success. The breeder is responsible for laying the foundation; the new family must build on that foundation. The selection of a family who will carry on the work begun by the breeder is the rest of the equation.

Both research and personal experience have led me to conclude that the families best suited for a pup would have as many questions for the breeder as the breeder has for them. The American Kennel Club's website (www.akc.org), lists the following questions that should be answered by every responsible breeder:

- How big will the dog get?
- How old will he be before he acts like an adult dog?
- How protective will the dog be?
- How often will the dog need to be groomed?
- How does he get along with other animals?
- How long can he be left alone at home?
- How much exercise does the dog need?
- What are the best training methods for this dog?
- What possible health problems might this dog develop?

Individual breeders may set specific priorities in selecting the families to whom they are willing to send their puppies. For example, the breeder of a line of outstanding show dogs may require an owner who is willing to make an effort to put a championship title on a particularly promising pup. However, there are certain standards that ALL breeders should set in screening potential families.

1. You must find families who have the time to work with the puppy. If the household consists of two working adults, who will care for this pup throughout the day while they are at work? Do their work schedules permit several trips home? Do they work from home during the day? Who will be the primary caregiver for this pup? Can they make arrangements to have someone come in to feed and walk the pup when they are at work?

2. The living quarters can greatly affect how the pup will continue to develop. Does the family live in an apartment or a house? Is the yard fenced? Where and how will the dog be exercised as a puppy and as an adult? Where will the pup spend most of his time? Where will he sleep? Where will he be when he is not being closely supervised? Where will he eat? Where will he potty?

3. Raising a puppy can become expensive. Does the family have the financial means to support the pup? The cost of proper nutrition, and routine veterinary care, and veterinary emergencies can

become a burden for a family not prepared for these expenses.

4. The family dynamics can contribute to the success or failure of having a new pup join the family. Are there children in the family? If so, what are their ages? Did you see the parents and children interacting? Were the children respectful and well-behaved? Did the children appear fearful of either parent or of the puppy?

5. Does the family have prior experience with dogs? Have they had experience with this particular breed? Why did they choose this breed? Why did they choose you as a breeder? Have they talked to other breeders? If so, why didn't they get a puppy from that breeder? If they have experience with dogs, how did they handle common training issues with their other dogs? Do they know a competent trainer who practices acceptable training techniques?

Each breeder must decide on the acceptable answers to these questions. Remember, a twelve-week-old pup requires a great deal of attention. Socialization is still in progress, which means many people to see, many places to go. The daily care includes several feedings and trips outside for potty breaks on a regular schedule. If the puppy is not kept on a schedule for feeding and potty breaks, he may develop bad habits that could lead to his being returned. Should this happen, the breeder will have to take time to re-housetrain him before he can be placed again.

Many families fail to comprehend the financial responsibilities required for the proper rearing of a puppy. More importantly, these same families may not be willing to accept this responsibility for the "family pet." You may want to ask questions regarding the kind of food they intend to feed the pup, or better yet, by *telling* them what kind of food, how much it costs and how much needs to be fed both as a pup and as an adult.

By this time, you have probably begun interviewing potential families for placement of your pups. It is a good idea to require the entire family to be present for your visits. Whether the visits take place at your house or at their house, this gives you an opportunity to observe the family dynamics. Be cautious of families wanting a dog to teach the children responsibility. When the child fails this lesson, what happens to the pup?

A family that has never had a dog is not necessarily a family that should be rejected, just as an experienced family is not always the best choice. I am reminded of one gentleman who wanted a pup from me. He was an experienced dog person, his children were well-behaved and respectful teenagers, the family was financially sound, he owned his own business, and the wife stayed home and was very excited about the idea of a new pup. They also had a large fenced yard where the dog could run and play. This seemed to be a perfect placement until I asked about their last dog. One of the children replied, "Our last three puppies were killed when they went under the fence." I told them to contact me again when they resolved the fence issue.

It is not a good idea to allow prospective families to pick from the entire litter. The breeder should use his knowledge of his bloodlines, his familiarity with the particular litter, and what he has learned about the family being considered to pre-select one, two, or three puppies to show the potential family. The breeder will select the puppy or puppies who best match the family's goals in seeking to acquire a puppy, their situation and the personalities of the various family members who will be in daily contact with the pup.

If you are a family searching for a puppy, you must trust and rely on the breeder's knowledge and experience. Presumably, you checked his reputation for integrity and reliability before you decided to look at his puppies. You need his expertise to help you find a match between your family's needs and the pup which best meets these needs. He may only show you the pups from which he is willing to allow you to choose. Either way, if you don't find the pup that you feel is right for you, don't choose one! There are other litters, and somewhere your puppy is waiting for you to find him.

No matter who the new family is (relative, friend or total stranger), always use a written contract. A contract states the terms of the sale so that there can be no question as to the responsibilities, obligations, and expectations of both the breeder and the new family. Another advantage of the contract is the fact that it can be revisited if clarification of any point is needed in the future. Included in the contract should be (a) the conditions under which the puppy must live; (b) the disposition of the dog in the event the family becomes unable or unwilling to provide for his care; (c) the health guarantees you offer and/or that you don't offer; (d) a list of health tests which were performed and the results of those tests or a statement declaring that you did not perform the health tests standard for this breed.

Each national breed club recommends certain genetic health tests for that particular breed. I strongly believe in conducting these tests. How the results are used is strictly up to the individual breeder. Some breeders choose to use only 100% clear dogs for breeding, while others may be forgiving with some tests. My concern here is that the puppy's family must be fully informed. Full disclosure of health issues is mandatory! If you choose to breed a dog that did not pass a particular test, you must inform the prospective buyer so that he is aware of the potential risk and financial responsibility he is assuming, as well as what limitation this may place if he wishes to use this dog in a breeding program. A responsible breeder will also include health information about any tests conducted on the siblings of the parents and on the grandparents and their siblings as well. Many responsible breeders may issue a "limited registration" if they feel that a dog should not be used in a breeding program, or if they prefer to wait until the pup is older before making a decision about the use of this pup to future the breed.

An excellent book that will assist breeders in understanding families, thereby helping the breeder to place their pups with the most appropriate family is Lynn Hoover's, *The Family in Dog Behavior Consulting*. Although the book is written for dog behavior consultants, it provides tremendous insight into the family dynamics as they relate to the dog.

One way to help insure the best for your pups is to require the reading of such classics of dogdom as Dr. Ian Dunbar's *Before You Get Your Puppy* and *After You Get Your Puppy*, both published by James and Kenneth Publishing and available at most dog-related e-bookstores. Many breeders provide a copy of *After You Get Your Puppy* to their new puppy families in their puppy kits. This book is a small expense that not only gives the breeder a more professional image, but also benefits the puppy that carries his kennel name.

The Breeder's Guide to Raising Superstar Dogs

Registries

The purpose of any registry is to keep the records of the breeding stock registered with the organization and to keep track of the competition events and the progress each dog makes. A number of people register their dogs with multiple registries. Some people do this in order to compete in a variety of events. I applaud anyone who competes in any event. I have dogs that are registered with as many as five organizations for competition purposes.

It should be noted that no registry can guarantee the quality of the breeding stock. A registry can guarantee only that the sire and dam are properly registered. However, the registration policies and standards of some registries are so lax that the registration is almost meaningless. Where breeding stock and puppy purchases are concerned, it is always the best course of action to stick with the more reputable organizations. As a rule, look for a registry that offers nationwide events throughout the calendar year, has well-organized breed clubs, offers many events in a variety of disciplines and is recognized and respected in other countries. Many people will associate the quality of your puppies with the quality of the registry that you choose.

Puppy Aptitude Testing

Puppy Aptitude Tests are frequently referred to as "puppy temperament tests," but they do not actually test or evaluate the puppy's temperament, which will not be fully formed until the pup is about fifteen months old. Puppy aptitude tests are useful tools that help the breeder to match a puppy's potential with the new family's expectations and agenda for their dog.

There is some debate about the most appropriate age for testing. Seven weeks (some say exactly 49 days old) seems to be the norm. However, pups mature at different rates, even in the same litter. This makes getting a true reading from any test challenging. It should be noted that the puppy that has experienced the social imprinting described and advocated in the previous section would react differently to aptitude tests than will a puppy that has not received the benefits of social imprinting. I have evaluated many litters that were isolated, with little or no contact with strangers. Those pups very seldom approached me without strong encouragement. Many pups never approached me! On the other hand, pups with social imprinting almost always approach the testers, and are glad to meet a stranger.

It is most important that someone who is a stranger to the puppies conduct the test in an unfamiliar environment. Many breeders do not consider it necessary to hire a tester; however, socialization is not about how the pups interact with the breeder, but with strangers. Furthermore, an evaluation from the breeder would be biased; a neutral tester's endorsement is much more valid.

A number of excellent tests are currently in use. The test I use consists of twelve sub-tests, which I have combined to focus on traits, that I believe indicate the probable development of adult characteristics. For example, if I see the propensity for assertiveness, problems may present later in life if this issue is not addressed. If the breeder uses this information to place this pup with an experienced family, this pup should develop into a well socialized, easily managed adult.

The puppy test should include at least two of each of the following: novel stimuli, puzzles that require the pup to think and solve problems, handling exercises in which the pup is picked up and handled, and tests in which the pup is required to work/interact with the tester.

While the pups are going through the series of tests, a scorer is recording the appropriate score for each test. Upon completion, the tester then reviews the scores and gives an evaluation for each puppy. An experienced tester will give written, detailed explanations of each pup's results. This information should be available to the new puppy owners in their puppy kits. The test sheet should include the entire litter with their puppy highlighted. Contact information for the tester should be listed.

Adult Temperament Testing

Adult temperament testing can provide a seal of approval on your breeding program. If you properly selected the sire and dam, followed the Superstar Program throughout the puppies' developmental stages, used sound judgment in properly matching the puppies with their new families, and educated the families on how to continue the skills development that you began, you should now recommend adult temperament testing for the dog. He should pass the test with flying colors!

The American Temperament Test Society, Inc. (ATTS) is the oldest temperament testing organization in the United States. As described on their website (www.atts.org), "The ATTS test focuses on and measures different aspects of temperament such as stability, shyness, aggressiveness, and friendliness as well as the dog's instinct for protectiveness towards its handler and/or self-preservation in the face of a threat."

Dog must be eighteen months old to be evaluated. Prior to beginning the test the person who will handle the dog is asked to complete a brief profile, which will be given to the testers. Based on this profile (which includes breed, age, sex, whether intact or neutered and certain life experiences), the testers will compare the reactions of this specific dog to the average or norm for a dog with similar characteristics and background. The perfect "average" score for the test is five. Scoring of the dogs reactions is rated from zero to ten, with scores in the four to six range considered average. A dog to whom two testers give a zero on the same sub-test will fail the test.

The test is conducted on a pre-set path where the dog/handler team will encounter ten sub-tests in which the dog will be exposed to various social, audio, visual, and tactile stimuli. Three independent testers evaluate each dog simultaneously. Incidentally, one of the factors that makes the ATTS test so reliable and respected is the standard of excellence required of the testers. Each tester must serve probationary periods under an experienced tester at several different levels and pass written tests before moving to the higher levels. It takes the average tester three years to advance to the tester status, and an additional four years to earn the title of Chief Tester.

Although ATTS does not require a dog to ever retake the test once he passes, I strongly recommended that with any change of living conditions or environment the dog be retested. A dog that passes may retake the test as many times as the handler desires.

Conclusion

For more than a decade, the Superstar Program has consumed me. Whether it was putting it into practice with my own litters, assisting other breeders in implementing it, or doing countless hours of research, this program has been my life. I am very proud of and very passionate about it.

As breeders, we must first start with sound genetics, breeding only dogs with sound temperaments. We must also prove our breeding stock by using the appropriate health testing. We must then provide the puppies with sound imprinting of the basic skills, and finally we must choose the best families for our pups. We must insure that these families have the financial means, the emotional means, the ethical frame of mind, and the intelligence to ensure that the dog is properly trained. This includes following up on the pup's development and providing ongoing advice for the life of the dog. Remember, the family with whom you place a pup with is becoming a part of your family. Make sure that you can live with that!

For many years now, trainers have been kept busy solving everything from simple sits and downs to complex behavior problems. In 1975, when I first started teaching obedience, the five most common problems were barking, pulling, jumping up, destructive behavior (chewing/digging), and aggression. Today, the five most common problems are barking, pulling, jumping up, destructive behavior and aggression. As a trainer, I see the same problems recurring over and over again. Granted, this has kept me financially comfortable for many years, and I probably should not complain. But if trainers are seeing the same issues with dogs again and again, then something is causing these issues between birth and the time the trainer sees the young dog. The bigger problem is, what about the dogs with issues that are not seen by the trainers, what happens to those dogs? Those dogs are still a part of the problem; they are the ones that end up in less than desirable situations. The common factor in all of these situations is the breeder.

Some of you who have read this book will use the Superstar Program in its entirety and will produce great puppies. Others will use parts of it, and will experience good results. As a bare minimum, should you choose not to use the full program, the four critical areas that should not be skipped are the Bio-Sensor, the imprinting of basic skills, the socialization, and certainly the bite inhibition. The other skills will make the dog a better family dog, working dog, will improve his confidence and his focus but will not impact his ability to survive as strongly as the above mentioned skills.

We live in an instant gratification, fast-food society today. We can prepare a complete meal for our family in under five minutes using a microwave oven; we can pull up to a speaker, give the voice on the other end our order, and our food will be handed to us once we "pull forward." We can see our photos the second we take them, and shortly thereafter, anyone in the world can view them on our web page. We have grown accustomed to this life. However, this approach will not work with our family and our family includes our dogs. If you follow the complete program, you will have a great deal of time invested in each puppy that leaves your home, but you will also have the satisfaction of knowing that you have done your very best for the puppy; you will have taken advantage of the opportunity to shape and mold the puppies' minds. That makes the time spent and the effort expended worthwhile.

We must learn to trust our dogs and more importantly, we must show our dogs that we can be trusted. As breeders, we have the perfect opportunity to develop young puppy minds; to shape and mold these innocent little creatures into a viable part of our lives. We can teach and show them that we are not here to harm them or to rule over them; we are here to work together with them in our society.

We are at a place in where we can put the information we have at our disposal into practice. YOU now have the knowledge to properly prepare puppies that you have assisted into this world; YOU now have the ability to adjust what is considered the norm; WE have it within our power to turn the pups of today into the **"Superstar Dogs"** of tomorrow.

About the author

I have been involved with dogs my entire life. When I was about twelve, I became interested in training when my father sent our family's German Shepherd away to be trained. On the first weekend when my Dad took me to visit Skip at obedience school, I was hooked. I just loved the atmosphere. I loved the dogs and I loved the training.

When I joined the Marine Corps in 1975 and was transferred to California, I took my personal dog, a Chow Chow named Bear to an obedience class. The instructor was impressed by my ability to work with my dog and asked if I would be interested in assisting her with her classes, an offer which I gladly accepted. Before long, I was teaching the simple skills, and by the end of the year, I was teaching classes on my own. Dog training has been a major part of my life ever since.

In the early 1990s, after almost twenty years of working on modifying behavior, I decided to try to find ways to prevent the behavior problems from arising in the first place. Behavior modification is certainly a necessary function for a dog with behavior issues, but perhaps there might be a way to "head these problems off at the pass" before they develop. After several years of researching what others had already concluded I decided to start at the very beginning of the dog's life, to look at what different breeders were doing with their litters. I had been exposed to the Bio-Sensor routine in the late 70s and had used it on occasion. After years of trial and error, I put together the program outlined in this book. This program has been used successfully on many different breeds, from large to small, with consistent results: confident, outgoing, well-mannered pups.

Using my version of imprinting, the "Superstar Program," I have bred Best In Show dogs, a breed winner at the Westminster Kennel Club show, and numerous AKC champions, not to mention many high-level competition dogs. Other breeders using all or part of my program have been equally successful.

I am a certified dog behavior consultant with the International Association of Animal Behavior Consultants (IAABC), a professional member of the Association of Pet Dog Trainers (APDT), and a professional member of the International Association of Canine Professionals (IACP). I have served on the Board of Directors of the American Temperament Testing Society, Inc (ATTS) and I am a Teaching Chief Tester with ATTS. I am also a certified PetTech Instructor, certified to teach pet first aid.

I am always interested in hearing from breeders who have had success using my program. If you have questions or stories about your successes, please share them with me. My email address is Jerry@k9fixer.com.

I am available for workshops and seminars. If your club or organization is interested in hosting a Superstar Dog seminar or workshop, contact me directly.

APPENDIX

Whelping box designs

One of the best things a breeder can do is to have a whelping box that is conducive to house training. I have seen several nicely designed whelping boxes. One of the designs was published in a book by Muriel Freeman, *The Complete Rottweiler.* Longtime Rottweiler breeder Clara Hurley designed the whelping box. Bill Sampson designed another. The drawing at the end of this section is of Bill's design. You can obtain the plans by contacting Bill. His email address is wbs00001@sambushed.com or you can visit his web site at www.sambushed.com.

The best feature of this design is an additional, but separate area. One area will be used as a living and eating area the other, a toilet area. This brings the house training idea to the forefront at a very early age and makes cleanup much easier for the breeder. It also makes the conversion to house training much simpler. The pups are raised in one side of the box. Once weaning has begun, at around three weeks, the other side will be used immediately following feedings. The pups finish eating and they are shuffled off to the other side. A change of floor texture helps the puppies differentiate between the living area and the toilet area, so a change in footing is important. Shredded newspaper works well, or better yet, a few squares of sod. This adds some realism to the picture, and imprints the toilet area into the pup's mind. This continues after every meal. Before long, the pups will go to the other side on their own.

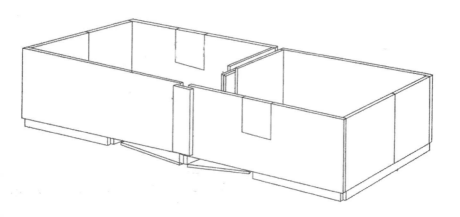

References

Seminars:

Dr. Ian Dunbar

Carmelo L. Battaglia, Ph.D.

Dr. Robert Van Hutchinson

Books and DVDs

Aloff, Brenda, *Positive Reinforcement: Training Dogs in the Real World.* Neptune City, NJ: T. F. H. Publications, Inc, 2001

Battaglia, Carmelo L Ph.D., *Breeding Better Dogs.* Atlanta, GA: BEI, 1995

Booth, Shelia with Dildei, Gottfried, *Schutzhund Obedience-Training in Drive.* Ridgefield, CT: Podium Publications, 1992

Bradley, Janis, *Dogs Bite But Balloons and Slippers are More Dangerous.* Berkeley, CA: James & Kenneth, 2005

Deeley, Martin, Working Gundogs, *An Introduction to Training and Handling.* Wiltshire, GB, The Crowood Press Ltd., 1990

Dunbar, Dr. Ian, *Before You Get Your Puppy.* Berkeley, CA: James & Kenneth, 2001

Dunbar, Dr. Ian, *After You Get Your Puppy*.
Berkeley, CA: James & Kenneth, 2001

Fogle, Bruce, DVM, M.R.C.V.S., *The Dog's Mind,*
Understanding Your Dog's Behavior. New York, NY:
Macmillan Publishing Co, 1992

Hoover, Lynn, *The Family in Dog Behavior*
Consulting. PA: Legand Publishing, 2006

Lorenz, Konrad, *Les Prix Nobel en 1973*. Stockholm:
Editor Wilhelm Odelberg, [Nobel Foundation], 1974

Reid, Pamela J, *Excel-erated Learning, Explaining*
How Dogs Learn and How Best to Teach Them.
Berkeley, CA: James & Kenneth, 1996

Rose, Tom & Patterson, Gary, *Training the*
Competitive Working Dog. Englewood, CO: Giblaut
Publishing Co, 1985

Scott, John Paul & Fuller, John L, *Genetics and the*
Social behavior of the Dog, the Classic Study.
Chicago, IL: The University of Chicago Press, 1965

Wilde, Nicole, *Help for Your Fearful Dog*, Santa
Clarita, CA, Phantom Publishing, 2006

Photography Credits

Unless otherwise noted here, all photographs were taken by and are the property of the author

Title page artwork by Robyn A. Alford

All German Shepherd pictures taken by Mary Alice Alnutt

American Bulldog picture provided by Mary Alice Alnutt

About the Author page photograph taken by Robyn A. Alford

Puppy Aptitude Testing photographs taken by Susan Tinch

Standard Schnauzer photographs courtesy of:
Crivitz Standard Schnauzers
Amy E. Shaffer
Crivitz, WI 54114
Conformation and Companionship
715-854-2356 / 715-927-5523
www.crivitzstandardschauzers.com

German Shepherd Dog photographs courtesy of:
Rainbow German Shepherds
John and Maggie Thomas
McDonough, GA
www.rainbowk9kennels.com

Rhodesian Ridgeback photographs courtesy of:
Mahaba Rhodesian Ridgebacks
Ann O'Mara
White, GA (Metro Atlanta)
(678) 493-4561
www.mahaba.info

American Pit Bull Terrier photographs courtesy of:
Mariah Henderson
McDonough, GA

- 157 -

Resources

DogStarDaily.com –

My favorite website in all of Dogdom

Dogwise.com –

My major source for dog educational material

The International Association of Animal Behavior Consultants (IAABC) – www.iaabc.org

Association of Pet Dog Trainers (APDT) – apdt.com

International Association of Canine Professionals (IACP) – dogpro.org

Horton's Handcrafted Quality Equipment

> Geneva, Georgia
>
> www.hortonsqualityk9.com
>
> (706) 269-3206

Happy Legs Stand-Stay Stilts

> Kennesaw, Georgia
>
> www.happylegs.com

Sounds Good CD's

> Legacy Canine
>
> www.legacycanine.com

Index